We'll meet again

Britain at War

We'll meet again
Britain at War

MAUREEN HILL

Photographs from the
Daily Mail

ATLANTIC WORLD

Britain's darkest and finest hour

This book deals with many facets of Britain at war, building up a collage of images to give a comprehensive picture of what the country looked like, what the people experienced and how they responded to what was a time of great individual and national trauma.

The photographs, restored to original condition, are drawn from the vast archive of the *Daily Mail*. Some were taken to accompany the news stories of the day; some to accompany morale-boosting features; others are obvious propaganda. A few were published at the time; some never got past the censor and others had instructions in the censor's blue pencil about what had to be blanked or cropped out, and what details the accompanying captions could tell, or not tell. Individually, each photograph tells a story and many in sequence form a compelling narrative. In addition the scribbled notes and typed captions on the rear of each photograph tell many interesting, fascinating, funny and tragic tales to add to the visual images.

These notes and captions have often found their way into the captions in this book, wholly or in part. The way in which they are written gives a vivid idea of the viewpoint at the time and often gives a strong sense of immediacy to the photographs they accompanied. Where this material has been used it appears in quotation marks. Sometimes a date has been added in brackets to indicate what 'today' or 'yesterday' meant in the original caption.

Each of the eight chapters opens with an overview of a particular topic – the 'Home Front' presents a detailed view in words and pictures of what everyday life was like for those in Britain during the war. Men's lives are portrayed principally in the 'In Uniform' chapter, as it was they who formed the bulk of the armed forces and the whole of the combat force. In 'Women in the Workforce' there is a focus on women's contribution to the war effort. And the experiences and contributions of children are detailed in 'A Wartime Childhood'. However, these chapters are not alone in cataloguing the lives and experiences of the population of Britain under the greatest threat to their way of life in a millennium – the whole book gives a comprehensive insight into the war, its opening, progress and the landmarks towards a British and Allied victory.

Through its memorable photographs and its detailed text, this book evokes a picture of people's daily experience and amazing courage under pressure. It is a testament to the spirit and hard work of the British people and the support they gained from their Allies in what was Britain's darkest and its finest hour.

CHAPTER ONE

War *is* declared

At the end of September 1938, Prime Minister Neville Chamberlain had negotiated a peace deal in Munich with Adolf Hitler, whose annexation of the Sudetenland area of Czechoslovakia had sparked an international crisis. Just 20 years since the end of the 'Great War' there was little appetite for another conflict with Germany that would embroil vast tracts of Europe. Thus, Chamberlain agreed that those parts of Sudentenland occupied by ethnic Germans could become part of German territory. On return from the talks in Munich he declared, 'I believe it to be peace in our time.'

However, this appeasement policy became increasingly futile and, following Germany's refusal to conform to an ultimatum to withdraw from the Polish territory it had invaded on 1st September 1939, the British people expected the worst. When Chamberlain broadcast to the nation at 11.15 a.m. on 3rd September it was to proclaim that 'this country is now at war with Germany'.

Waiting for the news

RIGHT: As it became clear that war was a likely consequence of Germany's refusal to withdraw from Poland, people gathered at Downing Street. Here police hold back the crowd on the morning of 3rd September.

BELOW LEFT: The Town Clerk reads the Royal Proclamation calling on all men up to the age of 36 to register for military service.

BELOW RIGHT: Soon after the declaration of war an air-raid warning sounded and people rushed for shelter.

OPPOSITE PAGE MIDDLE: Crowds in Downing Street on the morning of 3rd September as the declaration of war is made.

OPPOSITE PAGE BELOW: On 2nd September people had gathered in the streets around the Houses of Parliament to hear news of Prime Minister Chamberlain's speech to the Commons in which he was expected to deliver an ultimatum to Germany to withdraw from Polish territory. When he failed to do so the derision from MPs forced the Cabinet into late-night talks, from which discussions emerged a resolve to demand the withdrawal at 9.00 a.m. the following day, with an 11.00 a.m. deadline for compliance.

A *place of safety*

The threat and fear of aerial bombardment, first seen in the First World War and developed by the Germans in the Spanish Civil War, led to a mass evacuation of children, young mothers, pregnant women and vulnerable adults from the major cities to safe areas.

Such an evacuation was a huge logistical undertaking which was accomplished relatively smoothly. Nevertheless, the human cost of the project, for those evacuated, those left behind in the cities, and those that housed the evacuees, was significant, emotionally, practically and socially.

OPPOSITE PAGE: A kindly policeman helps a London youngster on to an evacuation train.

OPPOSITE PAGE INSET LEFT: A soldier carries a sleeping child to the train.

OPPOSITE PAGE INSET RIGHT: Carrying their gas masks in cases and wearing luggage labels to help identify them, this group of children from the Hugh Myddelton School in Clerkenwell were part of the first wave of evacuees who left London on the day Hitler invaded Poland, 1st September, 1939.

ABOVE: Smiling children wave as they begin their evacuation to the south-east coast in June 1940 during the Battle of Britain.

RIGHT: Mother and the baby of the family bid farewell to big sister who is off with her schoolmates on a train bound for Yorkshire.

Defenders for the home front

LEFT: Charles Remnant calls for volunteers to join the 'Citizen's Army' at a meeting held on Tooting Bec Common.

BELOW: The Citizen's Army hold their first parade on Tooting Bec Common, dressed in civilian clothes and 'armed' with sticks and umbrellas. It was intended as a defence force in the event of a German invasion.

OPPOSITE PAGE ABOVE: Local Defence Volunteers (LDV) on parade. The LDV was set up as Germany unleashed its blitzkrieg in Europe. In July 1940 the LDV changed its name to the Home Guard, which later became affectionately known as 'Dad's Army'. Many of those who joined up were older but had seen action in the Great War.

OPPOSITE PAGE BELOW: Local Defence Volunteers march at a parade ground in Balham. They are weaponless but some have LDV armbands and soldiers' caps.

'So much owed by so many'

The skill and bravery of the pilots and aircrew in the Battle of Britain saved the country from invasion and the sentiment of Churchill's testament to them – 'never in the field of human conflict was so much owed by so many to so few' – was shared by the nation. The focus on the air war in the summer of 1940 also bought time for the army to re-group and begin to re-arm. On 1st January 1940 two million men between the ages of 20 and 27 had been called up and most were still undergoing training while the retreat from France was taking place. Conscription for military service extended throughout the war to include adult men up to the age of 50, and in 1941 all women between the ages of 20 and 30 without carer responsibilities. Not everyone was expected to go into the fighting forces; many were sent to do essential war work in factories or administration, and from 1943 the 'Bevin Boys' were conscripted into the coal mines.

OPPOSITE PAGE TOP: Bullet holes from a Spitfire's machine guns can be seen peppering this plane's swastika symbol.

OPPOSITE PAGE INSET: The wreckage of this plane, brought down by anti-aircraft fire, was strewn across a railway line in south-east England.

OPPOSITE PAGE BELOW: Closely guarded by soldiers, this Luftwaffe fighter plane's good condition would reveal useful information about enemy aircraft design.

LEFT: 'The pilot of this Messerschmitt 109 fighter claimed three victories. Each of the white bars on the tail denotes one. The pilot was out to get his fourth on Saturday, but he met his match over south-east England. His squadron's crest carried the motto "Gott Strafe England", meaning "may God punish England".

BELOW: As civilian sightseers gather the military stand guard over this Messerschmitt 109 shot down in raids over Ramsgate.

CHAPTER TWO

The Blitz

The Blitz is probably the most vivid image associated with life on the home front during the Second World War. The idea that civilians were vulnerable to military attack from the air was relatively new; there had been attempts to use zeppelins to bomb London in the First World War, attacks that were largely unsuccessful and infrequent. By 1939, aircraft technology had seen major developments, and the Luftwaffe gained experience of mounting coordinated bombing runs during the Spanish Civil War, most notably at Guernica in 1937. For British civilians, the real Blitz covered a nine month period from September 1940 until May 1941, during which time 43,000 lost their lives. By June 1941 the Luftwaffe were needed to support the fighting on the Eastern Front that had opened with Germany's declaration of war on its former ally, the Soviet Union. However, this did not mean that Britain was safe from aerial attack.

First strikes

London was the focus for most Blitz attacks and the 7th September 1940 marked the first in a series of raids on the capital that continued for the next 56 days. At first, the Germans mounted sorties day and night but losses were large and after a week the Luftwaffe switched most of their operations to take place under cover of darkness. Up to the 15th September the bombing was part of Hitler's invasion strategy, which necessitated the destruction of RAF capability to attack German troop ships landing on the British coast.

OPPOSITE PAGE ABOVE: A downed fighter-bomber lies almost intact in this London street.

OPPOSITE PAGE BELOW: The wreckage of a tram car damaged in a daylight raid in Blackfriars Road.

LEFT ABOVE: A London trolley-bus, wrecked during a raid.

LEFT BELOW: RAF officers survey the wreckage of the engine and propeller of a Dornier which was brought down near a London station during a daylight raid.

Surveying the damage

ABOVE: Locals in a south-west London suburb shop as usual, despite the damage caused by German bombs in a raid the previous night.

LEFT: While the side of this house is blown away, on the first floor the kitchen range with its clock and horse statues on the mantel are untouched, and on the floor above the mirror has not even suffered a crack.

OPPOSITE PAGE ABOVE: Grose's sports shop in New Bridge Street was hit in December 1940; the blast blew bicycles upwards into the rafters.

OPPOSITE PAGE LEFT MIDDLE: Civilians survey the damage to the Ring Sports Stadium at Blackfriars, wrecked by bombs in October 1940.

OPPOSITE PAGE LEFT BELOW: Rescuing a valuable painting from the debris of a bombed-out building.

OPPOSITE PAGE BELOW RIGHT: An Eton boy moves his belongings after stray bombs dropped on the school in December 1940.

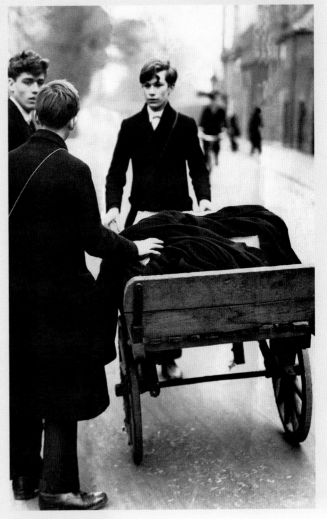

Attacking public morale

When Hitler's plans for a seaborne invasion on 15th September 1940 were thwarted by the skill and courage of the RAF, Luftwaffe bombing campaigns found a new rationale. The intention was that the death and destruction caused by bombing would severely damage morale, with the consequence that the population would urge the government to sue for peace; it was a policy adopted later in the war by the Allies. Thus, German attacks on London were designed as a symbolic blow to the capital of Britain, the Commonwealth and the Empire, while also seeking to damage the administrative heart of the country and disrupt the government's capacity to conduct the war effectively.

OPPOSITE PAGE ABOVE: A watchful guard stands amid the wreckage in Cloister Court within the Houses of Parliament; the damage came during a twelve-hour raid on London by 413 aircraft in December 1940.

OPPOSITE PAGE INSET: Fallen masonry lies on the terrace outside County Hall on the Thames embankment, after the building was bombed in September 1940.

OPPOSITE PAGE BELOW: Transport authorities had to deal with damage to the infrastructure as well as damage to vehicles. Here a railway bridge is wrecked.

RIGHT: Damage to this London bus was caused by falling masonry. Damage to London's buses became so severe that the authorities had to commandeer vehicles from outside the capital to keep services running.

BELOW: Another damaged bus – this time hit by a bomb dropped during a raid on 11th September 1940.

Salvaging belongings

OPPOSITE PAGE ABOVE LEFT: Part of the ground floor of Whiteley's department store, Bayswater, that was severely damaged in a raid in October 1940.

OPPOSITE PAGE ABOVE RIGHT: This house in a terrace row was demolished when a German bomb dropped on it.

OPPOSITE PAGE BELOW: As they salvage what they can of their belongings from the wreckage of their home, these Londoners are offered a welome cup of tea by a Salvation Army worker.

LEFT: The occupant of this home, Mrs Mann, managed a lucky escape when a bomb dropped on the rear of her cottage in outer London as she slept in her bedroom.

BELOW: 'Mrs M. Robertson and her family removing articles from their wrecked house.'

The Evening News
Three Famous Oxford-st. Stores
and Lambeth Walk Bombed

STATE
LONDON RED
A/C Approaching from In I AZ
LONDON WHITE
AIRCRAFT CASUALTIES
Period Sept. 15th 1940
ENEMY
DESTROYED 183 | PROBABLE 42 | DAMAGED 75
OUR A/C Pilots Safe 28

Avoiding 'deep shelter mentality'

In London, Blitz casualties were high with 13,000 killed and 20,000 injured during September and October alone. However, the availability of deep shelters in the London Underground system kept numbers lower than might have been expected. Tube stations became Londoners preferred shelters; initially the government were averse to the system being used for this purpose, in the belief that it would seriously hamper the Underground's ability to function and that it would foster a 'deep shelter mentality' in which the population of the capital spent long periods of time below ground, fearful of air raids. However, public demand and the clear evidence that the city and its people could still function as normally as could be expected, changed the authorities' minds.

OPPOSITE PAGE ABOVE: Auxiliary Fire Service (AFS) men pump water from the Thames to fight fires caused by incendiary bombs.

OPPOSITE PAGE MIDDLE LEFT: Cobblestones, dislodged by the bombing, provide another hazard to transport.

OPPOSITE PAGE MIDDLE RIGHT: Operations board from the War Cabinet HQ under Storey's Gate from where Churchill and the cabinet would conduct the war during raids on London.

OPPOSITE PAGE BELOW: East Enders queue patiently to enter air-raid shelters.

ABOVE RIGHT: The roof of the District Line tunnel was damaged in a raid in October 1940 but trains continued to run.

RIGHT: Troops cross a temporary road bridge over London's largest bomb crater, at Bank tube station. The immense crater was caused by a direct hit on 11th January 1941 that killed at least fifty people. The censor gave permission for this picture to appear in the newspapers on condition that all of the crater was blacked out, and only the road bridge, with the troops crossing it, was shown.

The Fire of London

OPPOSITE PAGE: One of the most devastating raids, resulting in what came to be known as 'the Second Great Fire of London', occurred on 29th December 1940. More than 10,000 fire-bombs rained down on the city on a night when the River Thames was at its lowest and enemy aircraft had earlier in the evening hit the water mains. The 20,000 firemen struggling with the blaze were reinforced by soldiers and civilians. Here the Pioneer Corps clear up around Tower Hill after the raid – the Tower of London can be seen in the background.

RIGHT: Workers gather outside their blitzed premises following the raid.

BELOW INSET: The ruins of a once busy street in Aldermanbury, near the Guildhall.

BELOW: St Anne's Parochial School, Hatton Garden ablaze as firefighters struggle to bring the flames under control on 29th December 1940.

New Year 1941

OPPOSITE PAGE ABOVE: The Guildhall suffered severe damage during the raid. Here, wreckage of the roof beams lies in the Banqueting Hall. It was to take years of careful restoration work post-war to return the building to its former glory.

OPPOSITE PAGE BELOW LEFT: On New Year's Day 1941, the Lord Mayor of London toured the ruins, here inspecting the damage in the Guildhall.

OPPOSITE PAGE BELOW RIGHT: The Lord Mayor at Aldermanbury, where the Wren church of St Mary the Virgin had taken a direct hit during the raid.

BELOW: The medieval walls of the Guildhall survived the Fire of London but the wooden roof, that was not as old as the walls, burned, the debris falling into the building.

St Paul's untouched amid the ruins

OPPOSITE PAGE ABOVE LEFT: The City from the west of the Old Bailey – Justice with her scales is just visible.

OPPOSITE PAGE TOP RIGHT: Taken a week after the Fire of London, this picture of St Paul's shows the ruins around the cathedral are still smouldering. One of the most powerful images of the war was captured on the night of the 29th December – it shows St Paul's standing untouched amid the flames and smoke. It was taken from the roof of the Daily Mail building by photographer Herbert Mason.

OPPOSITE PAGE BELOW: Although St Paul's escaped damage during the Great Fire, it was hit by German bombs during the course of the war. This crater in the north transept was made by a bomb dropped during a raid in April 1941.

BELOW: A view of the north side of St Paul's as the clear-up continues around the great building.

Legacy of the bombing

Following the Fire of London raid, the capital suffered almost nightly bombing until May 1941. During the night of 11th May over 500 Luftwaffe planes dropped hundreds of high explosive bombs and tens of thousands of incendiary devices. Many important London landmarks were damaged that night, including the chamber of the House of Commons and Big Ben. This was the last great bombing raid on London, but one of the legacies of the months of sustained bombing, a legacy that lasted for many years, was the fear of the attackers returning.

OPPOSITE PAGE: 'A postman tries to deliver letters in historic Watling Street, Roman highway, in the city of London, after the latest indiscriminate Nazi raid.'

RIGHT ABOVE: The Blitzed area around St Paul's, pictured in May 1943.

RIGHT MIDDLE: Thurston's, home of billiards, and the Automobile Association's HQ, that stand side-by-side in Leicester Square, were damaged when a bomb dropped on the area in October 1940.

BELOW: A London family made homeless by the bombing sit in the street awaiting a removal van.

Bombed out of home

LEFT: A fire hose lies amid the debris in Fetter Lane on 12th May 1941 after what was, in effect, the last significant raid on London in the Blitz.

BELOW: Families sit outside their homes in a South London street with all they have managed to save, following the bombing of the area.

OPPOSITE PAGE ABOVE: Salvaging belongings, while a nun offers some comfort.

OPPOSITE PAGE BELOW: Moving out of a bombed-out home in Hendon.

Raids on Southampton

BELOW: Dealing with people made homeless by raids on Southampton in December 1940.

LEFT: This family, made homeless when a bomb damaged their Westminster home in April 1941, are moving to a new billet in a '£100-a-week Park-Lane luxury flat.'

OPPOSITE PAGE ABOVE: In May 1941, amid the bomb rubble, office workers enjoy a basin of soup provided by the American Food Convoys.

OPPOSITE PAGE BELOW: Homeless children queuing for a free hot bath, a service, with free soap and towels, provided by Lever Brothers.

Bombs on Buckingham Palace

Lowering public morale was a key aim in the German High Command's bombing strategy. And it proved to be a frightening experience for many, and affected everyone's life. Nevertheless, while every member of the population was touched in some way, they did not become demoralised. In fact, the constant attacks seemed to provoke the reverse effect to that intended – the sense of a nation pulling together, for bombs did not discriminate, no one, not even the King and Queen who remained in Buckingham Palace for the duration of the war, was spared the effects, or the fear.

OPPOSITE PAGE ABOVE: When, in September 1940, five bombs dropped in the vicinity of Buckingham Palace, this crater outside the gates was caused by one of them.

OPPOSITE PAGE BELOW: The North Lodge, next to Constitution Hill, received a direct hit in a raid in March 1941. A policeman died when one of the stone pillars fell on him.

ABOVE: Workmen labour to repair another area of damage just outside the Palace gates, caused by the five bombs.

LEFT: A policeman shows off some of the wreckage caused by the bomb that destroyed the Palace's North Lodge.

OPPOSITE MIDDLE AND BELOW: Prime Minister Winston Churchill joins the King and Queen as they tour the wreckage at the Palace.

Coventry blitzed

A devastating attack on the ancient cathedral city of Coventry on 14th November 1940 was the first major raid on a town or city outside London. It marked a change in the tactics of the German High Command; not only were there to be attacks on the symbolic heart of the nation, but the destruction was to be spread throughout the country. The attack on Coventry was carried out by a squad of 500 bombers which dropped 500 tonnes of high explosives and 36,000 incendiaries in an attempt to set the city ablaze. The strategy was largely successful and although firecrews and emergency services worked tirelessly, by the morning Coventry's mediaeval cathedral was almost entirely reduced to rubble, along with around 50,000 buildings. A death toll of 568 civilians was reported.

OPPOSITE PAGE: Coventry Cathedral in November 1940 after the devastating raid on the fourteenth.

LEFT ABOVE: The burned-out interior of St Nicholas Church, Liverpool, which was hit by a number of incendiary bombs in a raid on 20th December 1940.

LEFT BELOW: A café and shops were wrecked when a bomb dropped on this unidentified north-east coastal town. People in the buildings were brought out when rescue workers dug a hole in order to access the basement.

Midlands raided

ABOVE: Amid the wreckage, the YMCA offer the bombed-out citizens of Coventry welcome cups of tea.

ABOVE INSET: Salvaging the contents of a home wrecked in a raid on Birmingham.

LEFT: MIDDLE: This was once a busy shopping street in Coventry.

LEFT BELOW: Less than 48 hours after the raid on 14th November 1940, the people of Coventry go about their business through the city's smouldering ruins.

OPPOSITE PAGE: On the night of 22nd November 1940, Birminham was subjected to an 11-hour raid. As a major manufacturing centre the city was an obvious target. Transport and telephone systems were severely affected but it was damage to the water system which caused the most urgent problem – firefighters had to rely on pumping water from the canals or leave some fires to burn themselves out. Here the struggle continues to extinguish the fire in this factory.

Sheffield hit

BELOW INSET: The Sheffield Blitz, on 12th December 1940, left Sheffield United's Bramall Lane stand wrecked.

RIGHT: Old Trafford football ground was hit during raids on Manchester.

BELOW: The damage to Manchester's city centre after the raids just before Christmas 1940.

OPPOSITE PAGE ABOVE: Virtually every tram car in Sheffield was left with some degree of damage – 31 were totally destroyed.

OPPOSIT PAGE BELOW: Like Manchester, Liverpool was blitzed in the week before Christmas 1940. Here, rescuers sift through the wreckage of homes.

Liverpool's Christmas Blitz

OPPOSITE PAGE ABOVE: Troops assist in clearing the debris in Sheffield after a major raid on 12th December 1940. Only three days later the city was attacked again. This was a frequent pattern in the Germans' bombing strategy – the raiders returned after a brief respite, just enough time to begin the clear-up operation.

OPPOSITE PAGE BELOW AND THIS PAGE ABOVE: Liverpool and the Birkenhead area suffered two nights of heavy attack on 20th and 21st December 1940. More than 200 people were killed in these raids. These pictures were taken after demolition squads had worked to make the city safe.

ABOVE INSET: A bomb crater in the back yard of a house in the North Riding of Yorkshire.

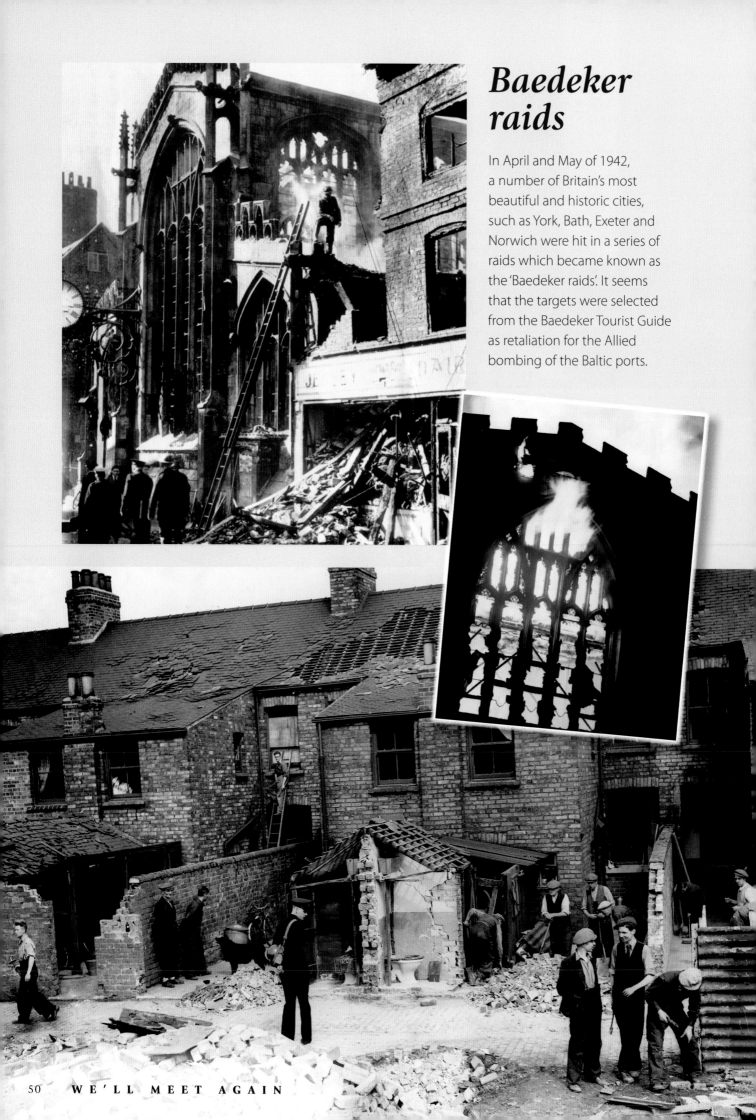

Baedeker raids

In April and May of 1942, a number of Britain's most beautiful and historic cities, such as York, Bath, Exeter and Norwich were hit in a series of raids which became known as the 'Baedeker raids'. It seems that the targets were selected from the Baedeker Tourist Guide as retaliation for the Allied bombing of the Baltic ports.

OPPOSITE PAGE ABOVE: A church in York after a Baedeker raid. Damage was severe in these provincial towns and cities as they had fewer air defences than other, more likely targets.

OPPOSITE PAGE INSET: York's 15th-century Guildhall in flames, after a raid in retribution for RAF attacks on Baltic ports.

OPPOSITE PAGE BELOW: Stray bombs demolished outhouses and brought slates from the roofs of these houses in a town in the North Riding of Yorkshire. Areas not designated as bomb targets were vulnerable to such random acts, as bombs fell accidently, or were jettisoned by bomber crews, or planes crash landed.

ABOVE: Middlesbrough Railway Station after a bombing raid in November 1942.

RIGHT: An air raid in Hull in July 1941 caused extensive damage in New Bridge Road, a residential district.

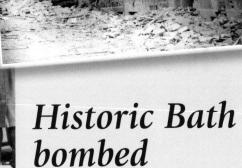

Historic Bath bombed

OPPOSITE PAGE ABOVE: The ruins of St Andrew's Church in Bath, gutted by fire after a Baedeker raid in April 1942.

OPPOSITE PAGE BELOW: A comic moment as Pioneer Corps come across a relic from the past in the rubble of bombed Bath.

ABOVE LEFT: 'The Luftwaffe have made yet another vicious "reprisal" raid on Bath. Swooping low in the moonlight, a demon Nazi plane dive-bombed and fired many of Bath's famous buildings for the second time, and sprayed the streets with machine-gun fire.
Photograph shows: Searching for victims in the ruins of St John's Roman Catholic Church which received a direct hit. One of the priests was killed.'

ABOVE RIGHT: Bomb damage to one of Bath's beautiful Georgian crescents.

LEFT: 'Thick grey dust covered the houses and roadway after the havoc caused in a Bath thoroughfare by Nazi raiders.'

Brief raid on Bristol

BELOW: Rescue workers carry away an injured man from the wreckage of a Bristol building bombed during daylight hours in a brief hit-and-run attack on 28th August 1942.

LEFT: An ARP warden stands amidst the wreckage of a church in the Birmingham area after a night raid.

OPPOSITE ABOVE: Damage from the daylight attack on Bristol in August 1942. As a major port and site of the Bristol aircraft factory, the town was subjected to some of the most severe attacks of the war, with the city centre almost completely destroyed.

OPPOSITE PAGE BELOW RIGHT: 'Firemen and rescue squads at work among the debris of houses wrecked by Nazi bombs during the large scale attack on a Midlands' town last night.'

OPPOSITE PAGE BELOW LEFT: Damping down the fires in the remains of a bombed-out church, somewhere in the south-east.

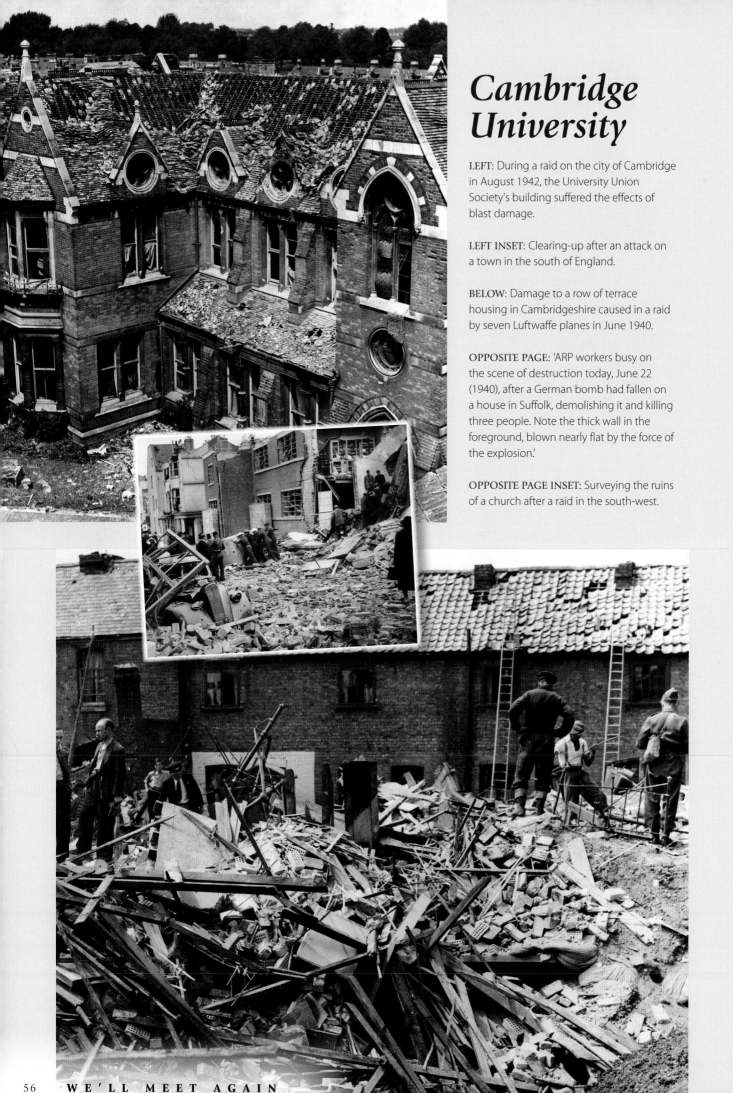

Cambridge University

LEFT: During a raid on the city of Cambridge in August 1942, the University Union Society's building suffered the effects of blast damage.

LEFT INSET: Clearing-up after an attack on a town in the south of England.

BELOW: Damage to a row of terrace housing in Cambridgeshire caused in a raid by seven Luftwaffe planes in June 1940.

OPPOSITE PAGE: 'ARP workers busy on the scene of destruction today, June 22 (1940), after a German bomb had fallen on a house in Suffolk, demolishing it and killing three people. Note the thick wall in the foreground, blown nearly flat by the force of the explosion.'

OPPOSITE PAGE INSET: Surveying the ruins of a church after a raid in the south-west.

Canterbury Cathedral

RIGHT: As a city close to the south coast, and on a bomber path from the continent, Canterbury suffered a number of air attacks, the most severe of which took place on 1st June 1942 as part of the Baedeker raids. The family pictured here, salvaging among the ruins of their home, were saved by their Anderson shelter.

BELOW: The Archbishop of Canterbury inspects damage to the Cathedral caused by the raid in June 1940.

ABOVE TOP: Firemen hosing down the smouldering embers of a building in the centre of Canterbury.

ABOVE: Amazingly, no-one was hurt when a bomb damaged this house in West Common Road, Hayes, Kent.

LEFT: '"Military objective". This is the Kent Hospital in which women patients were killed during the night raid. This picture shows you one of the two smashed wards. Among the debris Sister Gantry crawled, giving morphia injections to the injured women while rescue work went on.'

Exeter first Baedeker target

LEFT: The cathedral town of Exeter was the first to be targeted in the series known as the Baedeker raids. On 24th April 1942, following the first attack, a pilot in a German broadcast is alleged to have said, 'We will go out and bomb every building in Britain marked with three stars in the Baedeker Guide'. Here women and children walk through damaged Exeter streets.

RIGHT ABOVE: A bomb crater in the foreground shows how close the four people sheltering safely in the Anderson shelter (middle ground) came to being killed in this raid in the eastern counties.

RIGHT MIDDLE: 'Two women pick their way through debris in a badly battered street in Exeter.'

BELOW: Exeter's mediaeval cathedral rises above the surrounding damaged streets; apart from broken windows it escaped unscathed.

OPPOSITE PAGE: The bombed ruins of St Michael's Church in Great Yarmouth. The seaside town on the Norfolk coast was attacked frequently, especially in 1941 when it was raided on 167 occasions, destroying much of the ancient town.

Bombed bus depot

OPPOSITE PAGE ABOVE AND BELOW: Following an air raid on Dover on 23rd March 1942 that left 13 people dead, a demolition squad works to clear the damage and debris in this bus garage.

OPPOSITE PAGE INSET: Damage to housing in Dover during the March 1942 raid.

RIGHT: School boys sorting through the wreckage of their school after the devastating raid on Coventry on 14th November 1940.

BELOW: The spire of St Michael's Church rises above the ruined streets of Coventry a month after the raid.

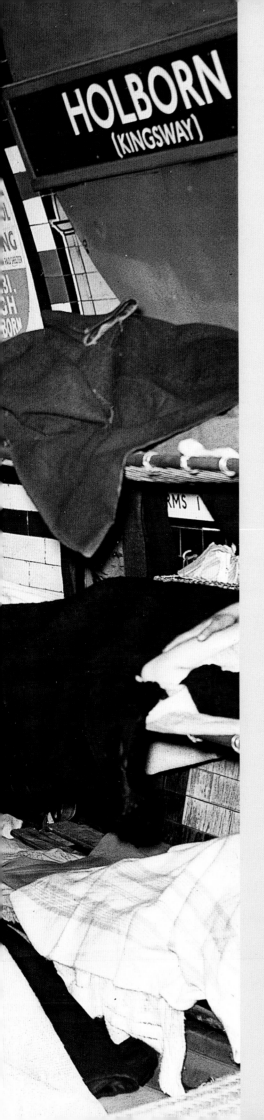

CHAPTER THREE

Defending the Home Front

Experience from the First World War and the Spanish Civil War alerted the government to the likelihood that aerial attack would make the British Isles a war front and that, even without an invasion, the risk of civilian deaths was great. Thus, from the early months of 1939 plans for civil defence were progressed. Air-raid shelters were delivered to thousands of homes and plans drawn up to evacuate children and other vulnerable people from areas thought to be at risk of bombing. Twelve regional Civil Defence Commissioners were appointed, with special powers to govern their areas should they become cut off from central government.

Resisting invasion

OPPOSITE PAGE: 'You are looking at the famous clock tower and the Houses of Parliament through a nearby barbed-wire entanglement – a symbolic picture that speaks of Britain's preparedness to withstand to the last any attempts at invasion.'

RIGHT: As part of a nationwide scheme to confuse any invaders landing in Britain by parachute, this village post office name sign is being painted over.

BELOW: Shortly after the retreat from Dunkirk, when invasion was a real possibility, there was an impetus to make Britain anonymous to invading troops. Painting out the name of this local railway station aided that anonymity.

Protecting buildings

LEFT: Workmen filling sandbags to protect Southwark Town Hall. Sandbags helped to mitigate against the damage caused by shock waves from a bomb blast.

LEFT MIDDLE: The owner of this restaurant was taking no chances. Shopfronts with their large expanses of glass were particularly vulnerable to damage. Covering shopfronts in a trellis work of sticky paper was a more common method employed to minimise the chance of flying glass.

BELOW: 'A busy sandbagging scene in the West End of London.'

OPPOSITE PAGE: 'Reporting for duty – this scout cycled around the district delivering messages between ARP posts.'

OPPOSITE PAGE INSET: Even the humblest of builings needed protection!

Bedding down in the tube

MAIN PICTURE: At the beginning of the Blitz in September 1941, Londoners sleep on the escalators in a tube station. Facilities were not yet set up to cater for those sheltering in the London Underground.

OPPOSITE PAGE INSET: 'The warden sees that the children are "comfy" in their hammocks at the Aldwych underground railway, now opened to the public as an official refuge.'

BELOW TOP AND BOTTOM: By January 1941, bunks had been installed on Underground platforms and passengers waited for the last train while others settled down to sleep. The deep tunnels of the Underground offered a safe haven, but even they were not entirely bombproof. In one of the worst incidents of the war 110 people were killed while sheltering in, or travelling through, Bank tube station when it received a direct hit.

BETTER 'OLE

PUBLIC SHELTER

PUBLIC SHELTER

City of Westminster 150 PERSONS
AIR RAID SHELTER

NOTICE
DANGER WARNING
WE DISCLAIM ALL RESPONSIBILITY FOR
DISAPPOINTMENT, AND DANGER TO LIFE
& LIMB, THAT MUST FOLLOW TO PERSONS
MISLED BY THE ABOVE NOTICE, WHICH WAS
PUT UP WITHOUT AUTHORITY FROM US.
OUR AIR RAID SHELTER IS REGARDED AS
INSUFFICIENT FOR OUR OWN STAFF.

Shelter etiquette

ABOVE: A warden stands at the entrance to a public shelter in London.

ABOVE INSET: 'Two conflicting notices posted outside the well-sandbagged premises of a firm in the Strand are attracting the attention of passers-by. The first, put up in the name of the City of Westminster, intimates that a public air-raid shelter for 150 persons is inside the building. The other notice gives the opposite view of the firm.'

RIGHT: A notice asking able-bodied men not to shelter in the Underground.

LONDON PASSENGER TRANSPORT BOARD

TO ALL ABLE-BODIED MEN

The trains must run to get people to their work and to their homes.

The space at the tube stations is limited.

Women, children and the infirm need it most.

Be a man and leave it to them.

Domestic shelters

LEFT: Although in an area subject to heavy bombardment and standing only 25 yards from where a bomb landed, this air-raid shelter, built from reinforced concrete, was undamaged. However, everyone knew that a shelter would not stand a direct hit.

BELOW: Some householders used their cellars as bomb shelters and it was necessary to ensure a emergency exit from the cellar in case the house above collapsed.

The blackout

In order to make it as difficult as possible for enemy aircraft to sight their targets blackout regulations were brought into force. All buildings were required to conform and in the early weeks of enforcement blackout materials sold out rapidly. Windows had to be covered so that no chink of light escaped; vehicle lights had to be dimmed and only project downwards; streetlamps were fitted with a special screen which dimmed their light.

The one thing cited most consistently as most inconvenient about the war was the blackout, and as patrolling the blackout was one of the major tasks of Air Raid Protection (ARP) wardens, they were often seen as 'nagging' about maintaining those regulations. However, their job was vital to the safety and security of the neighbourhood they covered. Wardens had to deal with the immediate aftermath of a bomb falling in their area, inform central control and organise ambulance, fire and rescue services. They would also be expected to administer first aid and to ensure that people remained calm at any incident.

LEFT: An ARP outpost in Essex where the blackout shade and desk lamps throw shadows into the room.

INSET LEFT: Demonstrating a mask for a car headlamp to dim and divert the light downwards.

INSET RIGHT: Shop window displays also need to reduce illumination.

ABOVE: A candlelight service at Christ Church, West Green, Tottenham, in response to the blackout regulations.

INSET RIGHT: Sometimes the blackout was carried to extremes. This is a 'pipe-smoker's shield – at each pull the glow from the pipe is reflected forward.'

RIGHT: A policeman demonstrates a red-light torch used to pull up any speeding motorist caught exceeding the newly established 20 mph limit in built-up areas – a measure introduced to ensure pedestrian safety when streetlights were dimmed during the blackout.

The Observer Corps

RIGHT: Two members of the Observer Corps on duty at sundown. Anti-aircraft units relied on the Observer Corps to signal the approach of enemy aircraft. Staffed by civilians, the corps was operationally controlled by Fighter Command. Full-time members worked 48 hours per week but many were part-time, working shifts in addition to other jobs.

MIDDLE INSET: A gunner carries anti-aircraft shells, ready for loading into the gun.

BELOW: 'An observer identifies a plane while his colleague plots the course.'

BOTTOM: Dawn breaks on an Observer Corps listening post.

Women in the corps

LEFT: Mrs Schofield and Mrs Fenwick, members of the Observer Corps, study books on aircraft recognition.

BELOW: 'Mrs Schofield is relieved at her post by her husband, also a Corps member, despite a full-time job as a draughtsman.'

Home Guard expertise

LEFT: A queue of men forms to join the Parachute Defence Corps at Loughton in Essex. As the Home Guard took over duties normally undertaken by regular soldiers, there was a need for such specialist units.

BELOW: In August 1940, with the real prospect of a German invasion, these men manufacture 'Molotov cocktails' for the Home Guard to use against German armoured divisions.

OPPOSITE PAGE TOP: The *Daily Mail*'s Home Guard unit on parade.

OPPOSITE PAGE BELOW: The company unit is inspected by Viscount Rothermere, owner of the *Daily Mail*.

Demolishing the danger

ABOVE: After London's first night raid in late August 1940, demolition squads work to make safe a damaged bank.

RIGHT: A demolition squad at work on a bombed house – one of the gang is working at the end of a rope making the roof safe. In the foreground another man works on a street lamp, many of which were still gas-powered at this time.

OPPOSITE PAGE TOP: Royal Engineers laying a gun cotton charge in preparation for a controlled explosion to demolish an unsafe wall.

OPPOSITE PAGE BELOW: A policeman cycles through a London street to signal the 'All Clear' after an air-raid drill in the first week of the war.

On home leave

ABOVE: This soldier is greeted by his family as he returns home on leave for ten days during April 1940.

RIGHT: The wedding of Private George Pinnock to Miss Joan Cox on 25th April 1940 at St Stephen's Church, Rochester Row, Victoria. The groom was on a 72-hour pass from his regiment, the Highland Light Infantry, and they were to see each other just once more in the next five years.

OPPOSITE PAGE: Two British soldiers, on leave from France, telephone home from the train station to announce that they have just got back to Britain.

OPPOSITE PAGE INSET: This soldier, greeted by two members of his family, was able to write home to let them know when he would be back on leave.

RAF glamour

The men of the RAF had the most glamorous profile of all the services. Their uniforms were more attractive in cut and colour and the tasks they were asked to carry out generated connotations of danger, heroism and romance. In 1939 the RAF was only 21 years old, having been formed at the end of the First World War from the Royal Flying Corps when air warfare was in its infancy. Just as it was a young service, many of the men were also young. But there was no disguising the danger – from the approximately 600,000 men who served 150,000 were killed. It was the service which became the front line in the Battle of Britain, after the army's retreat from Dunkirk, and the service which scored the first notable victory against the enemy.

MAIN PICTURE: 'The crew of a bomber have a few moments rest on the tender of bombs which will shortly be loaded onto their machine, to be dropped on some specified objective in Germany'.

INSET ABOVE: Ground crew from the navy's Fleet Air Arm at work on a new Vought-Sikorski 'Chesapeake' dive-bomber, nicknamed the 'cheesecake' by the men. The bomber, designed and made in the USA, was made available to Britain under the Lend-Lease Agreement, made in March 1941.

INSET BELOW: Pictured during the Battle of Britain, this crew had just returned from helping to repel a 100-plane-strong Luftwaffe attack.

Resting between sorties

OPPOSITE PAGE ABOVE: RAF pilots sleep and play games in their rest room at their base 'somewhere in Scotland'.

OPPOSITE PAGE BELOW: 'The men of the RAF Fighter Squadrons are ever on the alert, whether at work or during their brief hours of relaxation. This picture, taken at the County of London Squadron of the Fighter Command, shows the spirit which prevails amongst these men at all times and which has spurred them on to render their unforgettable service to their country.'

ABOVE: As they rest between sorties during one of the biggest battles of the Battle of Britain, squadron members listen to the account of a New Zealand flyer who had to bail out when he was shot down.

ABOVE: RAF cyclists carrying food to feed Barrage Balloon crews. Most of the Barrage Balloon sites were without catering facilities and so food was prepared at a central depot and then transported in hay boxes which kept everything piping hot, even over distances of 10 miles.

Jeeps hit London

ABOVE: American troops drive through central London in a 'jeep', described as a 'baby reconnaissance car'.

RIGHT MIDDLE: GIs stationed in a rapidly erected hut, on a USA Army camp in the Home Counties, built to house the growing numbers of American troops stationed in Britain.

RIGHT: Armed with a carbine, a US soldier stops a bus in a London street in May 1944 .

Making friends

ABOVE: Two women in Trafalgar Square are snapped by an American soldier.

RIGHT MIDDLE: This American soldier cycled to Ascot and worked alongside a local to pick the winners.

RIGHT BELOW: Joan Clarke, of the National Fire Service, offers a light to a newly arrived American soldier, Sergeant Frank Dardanell from Verona, Pennsylvania.

CHAPTER FOUR

Women at work

When the war started there was a necessity for labour on all fronts. Pre-war the workforce was largely male, but many of those men were required for the military. By 1940 Britain had three and a half million men in the armed forces. However, there was a need to keep essential services, like power and transport, running and a need to produce the munitions necessary to fight the war. The war itself created a large number of new jobs, from ARP wardens and fire spotters to demolition crews. Other jobs, like those in the fire service, required an increase in numbers to deal with the effects of war on civilian life. Women were the only pool of labour from which to recruit to breach the shortfall caused by the loss of so many male workers. To this end Winston Churchill, in January 1940, when First Lord of the Admiralty, called for a million women to help with war work, principally in the production of munitions.

Getting into the workforce

'Women of Britain – come into the factories' is one of the most well known slogans from the propaganda posters of the war but the majority of women in pre-war Britain had never worked in a factory; indeed few women had paid employment. It would not be unusual for a woman to marry and move from the parental home to living with her husband never having had a paid job. Those who did work outside the home normally left as soon as they married; many employers would not hire married women. Even though women in the First World War had gone into the workforce to aid the country, social convention, reinforced by the depression of the thirties, re-established the idea that paid employment was for men, the 'breadwinners' in the family.

Women responded to the calls for them to 'come into the factories' as well as taking on numerous other jobs: driving buses, glazing bomb-damaged windows, mending roads, delivering the post, working as shop assistants, being part of a demolition team, to name but a few. The diverse range of jobs undertaken by women, while not contributing directly to the war effort, were essential in maintaining morale and keeping the country run smoothly.

OPPOSITE PAGE: Mrs C. Miles of Mill Hill was employed by Hendon Council as a street sweeper.

OPPOSITE PAGE INSET: Miss Birdie Mahoney trains as a bus conductress in Cambridge.

RIGHT: 'Miss Bambridge, of Coombe Hill, took a job as a butcher at Kingston-on-Thames.

BELOW RIGHT: Conductresses on the Brighton trolley bus service set a national record with an absentee rate of less than one per cent.

BELOW MIDDLE: 'A trousered girls cleaning the window of a London teashop. With many thousands of men now in the Services, a good many of their jobs have to be carried out by women.'

BELOW LEFT: A woman paints replicas of the goods sold inside on to the boards that cover the bomb-shattered windows of this clothes shop.

Conscription

When Winston Churchill called for a million women to help with war work, it was only one of many calls for women workers, and although many responded to these calls, the country could never quite fill the labour gap. In December 1941 women between the ages of 20 and 30, described as 'mobile' – that is, they had no pressing responsibilities in the home – were conscripted to do war work, either in the forces or in industry. The age for conscription was extended throughout 1942, so that by 1943 nine out of ten single women and eight out of ten married women with children over the age of fourteen were either in the forces or in 'essential work'. Even women classed as 'immobile' took on part-time jobs outside the home or became 'outworkers', a role that involved making or assembling small machine parts in the home.

OPPOSITE PAGE ABOVE: Two women model post office uniforms – the inclusion of a trousered uniform was hailed as a first.

OPPOSITE PAGE BELOW LEFT: Offering comfort and refreshments to children being evacuated by train.

OPPOSITE PAGE BELOW RIGHT: Women sort parcels at Mount Pleasant Post Office, Christmas 1940.

ABOVE: 'The tricycle girls start out on a day's work.' These women are delivering towels to City offices.

ABOVE INSET: A postwoman delivers the Christmas mail. Women were employed to help with the increased mail. They were not given uniforms but wore their own clothes.

OPPOSITE PAGE: By September 1941 many women were full employees of the Post Office, and this woman makes the afternoon collection from a City postbox.

Munitions workers

The production of munitions
included not only the building of war
machinery but also the manufacture
of bombs, shells, mines and bullets
used by that machinery. Hundreds of
women were employed in producing
the casings for these items, a task
which involved working with
smelting furnaces and hot metal.
Once cast, the casings were sent to
be filled in other factories, usually
sited out of town because of the risk
of explosion. In order to minimise this
risk, women working with explosives
wore a cloak and beret of undyed
silk and rubber galoshes, and had to
remove jewellery, corsets, hairpins
or anything metal which might cause
a spark.

ABOVE: Manufacturing 'Sten' guns at the
Royal Ordnance factory in Theale, Berkshire.

ABOVE RIGHT: One of ninety training
at the Beaufoy Institute in Lambeth, this
young woman is learning how to use
measuring calipers. The women had all
paid £1 2s 2d (about £1.11) for a twelve-
week course.

OPPOSITE PAGE ABOVE: Miss Josephine
De La Porte, an evacuee from Jersey, is
pictured making shells at a munitions
factory.

OPPOSITE PAGE BELOW: 'Girl workers
in the Bottling Department showing the
shells being shaped and laid out to cool.'

Heavy work

LEFT TOP: In January 1941, Britain's first dustwomen assumed their roles in Ilford. The council employed 'eight comely dustbin-emptiers'.

BELOW LEFT: 'Mrs Flannigan, a woman bricklayer, works to repair bomb damage to a Southern Railway arch in London.'

BELOW RIGHT: Two women install a gas cooker. At the gas works, women took on a range of jobs, from installation and maintenance of appliances to heavy labouring jobs such as filling 100-ton coke sacks.

OPPOSITE PAGE TOP: 'Women in the "Pick and Shovel Brigade". At a new aerodrome somewhere in East Anglia about 100 women and girls are doing navvies' work with zest and enjoyment. Here they are laying pipes for drainage each side of the runway.'

OPPOSITE PAGE BELOW RIGHT: 'She-navvies cheerfully wheel barrow loads of heavy stones at a railway goods yard. Women can no longer be called the "weaker sex" for all over Britain they have answered the call and taken on jobs which were previously exclusive to men. The toughest of these is surely that of "Women Navvies" a classification which includes a multitude of rough, heavy or dirty jobs.'

OPPOSITE PAGE BELOW LEFT: These women, here filling sandbags, were the first to be employed to clear air-raid debris and help make buildings safe.

'Land Girls'

Food production was another area that needed to recruit a large workforce. The Women's Land Army, members of which were nicknamed 'Land Girls', formed the backbone of the body of women engaged in the cultivation of the land and rearing of meat. Many other women factory workers, along with schoolchildren, the forces and men in reserved occupations, helped out on the land by taking advantage of schemes that gave a holiday on a farm in return for a payment of several hours' labour.

ABOVE: One of 'three girls of the Women's Land Army ploughing reclaimed land on a farm in Bedford, with the aid of three tractors working in echelon.'

RIGHT: This picturegraph was distributed by the Ministry Of Information in 1944. The statistics show that more workers were needed on the land than before the war. This was because Britain had to produce more of its own food and, as a result, 200 per cent more land was brought into production.

OPPOSITE PAGE TOP: In 1944, a Land Girl ploughs a field in southern England, wearing a tin helmet to protect her from the debris from flying bombs brought down by RAF fighters.

OPPOSITE PAGE BELOW RIGHT: Land Girls Margaret Gower and Mary Rigg (with 'Doodlebug' painted on her helmet) shelter from an overhead battle to bring down flying bombs.

OPPOSITE PAGE BELOW LEFT: Daisy Beales, a farmer's daughter, clears land with a billhook.

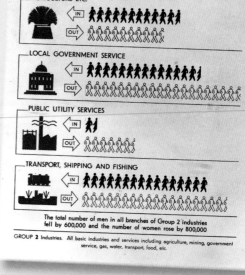

The part played by women in Britain's war effort

REPLACING MEN

4 examples from Group 2 Industries

Each BLACK symbol represents 10,000 women added
Each WHITE symbol represents 10,000 men withdrawn

AGRICULTURE ETC.

LOCAL GOVERNMENT SERVICE

PUBLIC UTILITY SERVICES

TRANSPORT, SHIPPING AND FISHING

The total number of men in all branches of Group 2 industries fell by 600,000 and the number of women rose by 800,000

GROUP 2 Industries. All basic industries and services including agriculture, mining, government service, gas, water, transport, food, etc.

In the early weeks of the war this garage proprietor ensured the petrol supplies were safe from the bombing with a liberal stacking of sandbags.

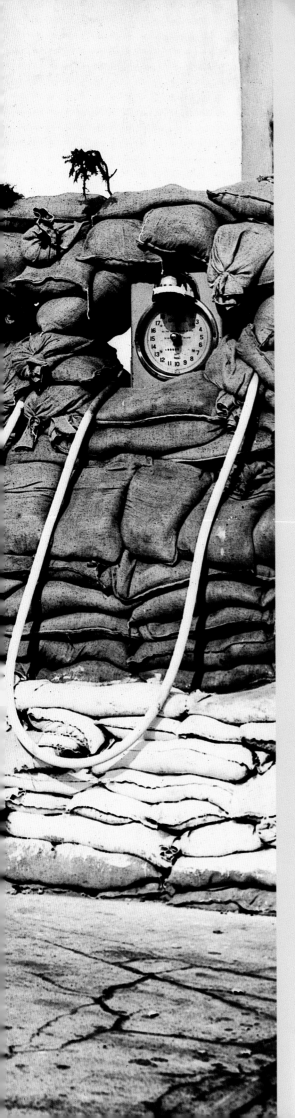

CHAPTER FIVE

Working for the war effort

During the war, everyone, whether young or old, rich or poor, male or female, experienced at some stage, and to varying degrees, a life of unremitting toil, privation and loss. Complaints about conditions were frequently greeted with: 'Don't you know there's a war on!' The war effort required everyone's energy, through military service, paid employment, voluntary work or running a home. Through the effects of bombing, or the need to commandeer houses to accommodate military personnel or evacuees, some lost their homes and often their way of life. Everyone financed the war through their taxation and savings schemes which targeted everyone, even children. However, there was little to spend money on as there was insufficient spare manufacturing capacity in the country to produce luxury items, and imported goods and raw materials put the lives of merchant seamen at risk of attack from German battleships and U-boats.

Munitions

Once the government had established a military force, its next priority was to organise the production of the munitions with which that force could fight the war. Factory space, a labour force and raw materials were needed to produce munitions. Some raw materials were imported but many were provided by 'salvaging' or recycling items already in the country. Teams of women and children, organised by the Women's Voluntary Service (WVS), toured from house to house, collecting metal in the form of tin baths, saucepans and old tin cans. Additionally, they collected scrap rubber, rags, waste paper and old animal bones, all of which had some use in the production of weaponry.

OPPOSITE PAGE TOP: Inspecting shells at a Royal Ordnance factory. Quality control was very important in order to prevent the military being put at risk from its own equipment.

OPPOSITE PAGE MIDDLE: Men at work in the torpedo workroom.

OPPOSITE PAGE BELOW: Inspection was carried out at all stages of production. Here the cases for naval shells are checked.

RIGHT TOP: Storing torpedoes in an Admiralty factory. Each torpedo contained more than 6000 parts and took several months to complete.

RIGHT BELOW: Every torpedo was 'tried out' and 'passed under working condition' before being dispatched to a Royal Navy ship.

Rifles

ABOVE LEFT: Rifles being stacked ready for dispatch. Photographed during the week of the retreat from Dunkirk, there was useful propaganda in ensuring that the public understood that, despite the fact that the soldiers had to leave most of their equipment behind, there were plenty more weapons in stock.

ABOVE RIGHT: Piling up rifles to service the British Expeditionary Force (BEF) in November 1939. The BEF had joined with French troops to prevent any further German advances.

LEFT: A factory inspecting room which was 'working at emergency pressure, day and night, to produce small arms, spare parts and tools.' Britain had not spent money on armaments in the years after the First World War and consequently when war broke out again it was a race to provide the equipment the military needed.

OPPOSITE PAGE: Thousands of empty cartridge cases ready for filling.

Building bombers

LEFT: A production line for the Blenheim bomber, 'whose speed and range', it was claimed, had 'outclassed anything the Germans have'. This was just one of the several aircraft factories around Britain producing fighter and bomber planes.

RIGHT: 'Your flying saucepan is doing just fine. The thousands of tons of aluminium pans that housewives gave up to the Ministry of Aircraft Production are making first-rate Spitfires. Smelting factories where saucepans, preserving pans and kettles are being turned into ingots for the plane factories are working at full pressure. Men, stripped to the waist, work in an atmosphere as warm as Kew Gardens' hothouse. Day and night, and through air raid warning, they shovel your household ware into furnaces and it comes out a flowing, white-hot liquid. The photograph shows men stacking pure ingots of aluminium to dispatch to the Aircraft Presses.'

BELOW: Anti-aircraft guns on the production line in a Midlands factory.

ONE MONTH'S RATION FOR FOUR PEOPLE—ONE OVER 70 AND TWO CHILDREN.

EXTRA RATION

EXTRA RATION

TEA ¼ lb.

TATE & LYLE SUGAR

MARGARINE 4 lb.

MARGARINE 2 lb.

TEA 2 lb.

SUGAR 8 lb.

LARD 2 lb.

TATE AND LYLE SUGAR

BUTTER 2 lb.

SWEETS 1 lb.

EXTRA RATION

We regret that the Food Regulations do not permit the sale at this branch of Rationed Goods (other than Cooked Ham) to Customers registered at other Sainsbury branches.

NEWCASTLE CO-OPERATIVE SOCIETY LIMITED

Name ....

Address ....

....

Pass Book No..

Number in Household..

C.P.S. N/o.

	WEEK ENDING:							
	Nov. 11th	Nov. 18th	Nov. 25th	Dec. 2nd	Dec. 9th	Dec. 16th	Dec. 23rd	Dec. 30th
BUTTER.. .								
BACON or HAM .. .								
SUGAR .. .								

On the ration

OPPOSITE PAGE TOP: As early as January 1940 the first food rationing came into effect. This photograph does not represent all of the ration, as fresh milk and meat were also included. Foods such as bread, fish, offal and fruit were 'off the ration' but they were often in short supply.

OPPOSITE PAGE BELOW LEFT: As the war progressed more types of food were rationed. On 8th February 1943, tinned fruit came under the 'points' system which allowed people to purchase items, most often those deemed luxuries, in addition to the basic ration. There was some choice, for example tinned plums instead of tinned peaches, but there were still restrictions on the amount one could purchase.

OPPOSITE PAGE MIDDLE RIGHT: Collating coupons for the second issue of ration books. 'Machines costing thousands of pounds were installed for the new printing. The coupons were printed on strips of paper 8 in. wide. The full run of 50,000,000 books used 35,000 miles of it.'

OPPOSITE PAGE BELOW RIGHT: Staff in the Money Order Department at the GPO (Post Office), where the savings of millions of people were administered.

ABOVE: This shop assistant cuts the coupons from his customer's ration book. As the sign on the shelf states, it was only possible to buy rationed goods in the shop with which you were registered.

ABOVE INSET: This 'ration book', issued to members of the Newcastle Co-operative Society in November 1939, before official rationing, was probably a response to shortages. Butter, bacon, ham and sugar, the first items to be rationed when the official system came into effect, are the focus of this rationing system.

Making do

Food, clothes and petrol were all rationed; even soap was rationed and no one was allowed to have a bath more than five inches deep, in order to conserve fuel and the pressure on the water systems. If something was not rationed then the chances were that it was in short supply or simply unobtainable. People had to 'make do and mend', rescuing worn or broken items, and find inventive solutions to replace those items in short supply – constructing a baby's cot out of an old drawer, experimenting with mixtures of face cream and shoe polish to colour stockingless legs, making children's clothes out of cut-down adult clothing.

ABOVE: In June 1941 clothing rationing was introduced, using a points system. Originally 60 points per year were allocated to eveyone to be spent as wished. Later the points allocation was reduced to 48. Selfridges responded to the news of clothing rationing by setting up an enquiry desk to help answer customers' queries.

LEFT: A customer buys shirts with margarine coupons which, when clothes were first rationed, could be used if the buyer had not been issued with a clothing ration book.

Queues for everything

As everything was in short supply people spent hours queuing for food and goods. The government controlled prices in an attempt to avoid profiteering. Some shopkeepers kept unrationed items 'under the counter' to sell only to regular customers. There was also a black market, which was illegal and often involved those who had been on the wrong side of the law before the war.

ABOVE: A queue in Kentish Town for the greengrocer's in July 1945. Despite the victory in Europe there was no sign of an improvement in supplies.

RIGHT: Queuing for fish in Streatham High Road in July 1945.

BELOW: A fish queue in Hammersmith in June 1945. The fishmonger was able to supply the fish but customers had to bring their own paper in which to wrap it.

Fuel rationing

ABOVE LEFT: Vehicle fuel was reserved for the military and other transport necessary to the war effort. It was only available to members of the public for 'essential' journeys – a doctor doing his rounds in a rural area, for example. Most cars were out of action for the duration of the war.

ABOVE RIGHT TOP: Apart from a few buses for late-night workers, a 10.00 p.m. curfew was imposed on London's buses. Although the main reason was to preserve lives during the Blitz, it had the added advantage of saving fuel.

ABOVE RIGHT BELOW: In response to the lack of petrol for motorised taxis, an old fashioned 'growler' cab, driven by horse power, made an appearance on London's streets.

LEFT MIDDLE AND BELOW: Increasing numbers of horses were seen on Britain's roads for all manner of jobs, mainly transporting goods.

OPPOSITE PAGE TOP: 'With petrol rationing and motorists laying up their cars, horses are coming into their own again. And street scenes resembling more and more those of days gone by. Compare this picture in Piccadilly yesterday (5th October 1939) with the scene in 1891 (inset right).'

OPPOSITE PAGE BELOW: 'First day of petrol rationing (25th September 1939) – and this was the scene yesterday on a by-pass road near London which is usually crowded with speeding cars. People ambled pleasantly on horseback or bicycled gaily by, but for the greater part of the day there was not a car to be seen.'

Dig for victory

TOP: The development of allotments was encouraged and by 1943 there were 1,400,000. Additionally, parks and open spaces were turned over to growing food; golf clubs, tennis courts, grass verges and the moat of the Tower of London were all utilised. Here a Mr and Mrs Flack 'dig for victory' on Clapham Common.

ABOVE LEFT: Maureen Copeland helps her dad prepare the soil on their plot on Clapham Common.

ABOVE RIGHT: Winifred Chapman shoulders her spade, ready to work on Clapham Common.

OPPOSITE PAGE TOP: Britain needed to be able to produce as much food as possible and the 'Dig for Victory' campaign encouraged people to grow their own. Often this would provide the majority of a family's fresh fruit and vegetables. Here schoolchildren in Monmouthshire tend vegetables in the school garden.

OPPOSITE PAGE MIDDLE: For many families with men away in the forces it was not possible to keep an allotment. Mrs Mann and Mrs Padwick, pictured here surveying the allotments in Hyde Park, were just such cases. Produce of other allotment workers' labour would contribute to the diet of these families.

OPPOSITE PAGE BELOW: 'There is a prosperous farm about a quarter of an acre in extent, tucked away under the shadow of St Giles, Cripplegate, which was damaged in the 1940 air raids. Firemen from the station across the way made it, almost everything there, except the livestock, was provided by the blitz. The bricks for the pigsties came from bombed buildings, so does the wood from which the fowl-houses and the "tomatory" are made. On it there are almost every vegetable known to gardeners, and six apple trees, reputed to be the only apple trees in the City.'

CHAPTER SIX

Growing up at war

For many children the six years the war lasted encompassed the bulk of their childhood. Paradoxically, while it was a time of danger and fear, of dislocation and loss, it was also a time of unprecedented freedom for many children, and the community spirit arising from the privations of war made them feel secure. Children were also encouraged to contribute to the war effort, and did so in many important ways.

Early evacuees

Images of evacuation are those that spring most readily to mind when we think about children during the war years. Even before war was declared, the official evacuation schemes began. As part of the process, Britain was divided into three sorts of areas: evacuation, reception and neutral. Evacuation areas were those in danger of bombing, principally in large cities and areas of industrial production. Reception areas were situated in country towns and villages considered safe; here people were expected to offer billets to those from evacuation areas. No one could leave, or be evacuated to, neutral areas.

ABOVE: Carefully carrying their gas masks, these East End schoolchildren leave London for their evacuation destinations on the day before war was declared. Some parents had taken the decision to evacuate their children privately – often abroad to places like Canada. However, the official evacuation did not begin until 30th August 1939.

ABOVE INSET: Evacuees board a bus at Edgware Station on 1st September 1939. Although still officially the summer holidays, children reported to school. They left with only the belongings they could carry, labelled and accompanied by teachers.

RIGHT: 'The Lost Worshippers. This picture was taken yesterday at a church a few yards from the London school bombed in the day raid last week. A week before nearly 200 attended the service. Now the pews are empty but for a few children who survived the Luftwaffe's attack.'

OPPOSITE PAGE TOP: A convoy of buses on the Kingston bypass, carrying schoolchildren to a mainline station for evacuation by train.

OPPOSITE PAGE BELOW: Children asleep on the floor of their classroom. They had gathered there the previous day to be registered and processed. They slept overnight at school, ready for their evacuation journey the following day.

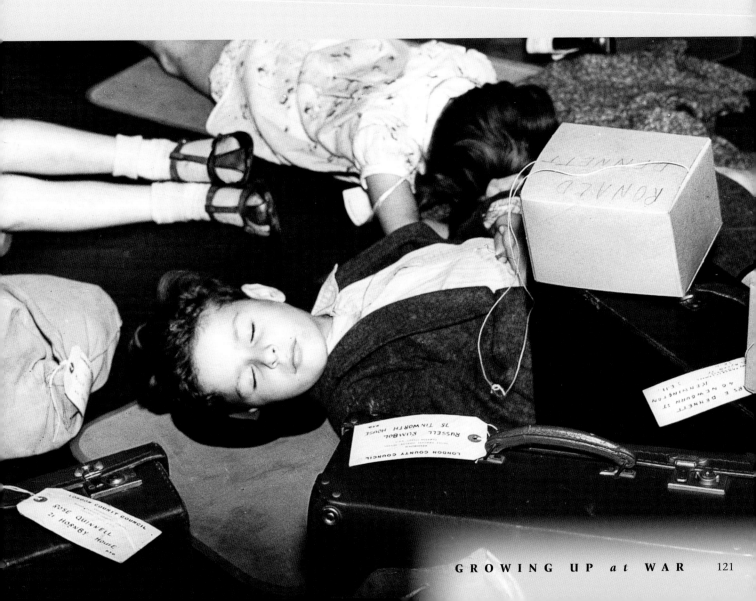

Town meets country

Evacuation was the major impact of the war on many children's lives. Often the clash of cultures between children from the city and their hosts in the countryside was a source of problems for all concerned. Children from the poorest areas in the major cities frequently lived in deprived conditions, often without access to running water. Consequently, they were often unwashed and prone to minor infections such as scabies and impetigo. While this shocked many host families, most were understanding and worked hard to accept the evacuees into their homes. Sometimes the difference in standards was the other way round and children with baths and electric lights at home found themselves staying in farm labourers' cottages without running water or electricity.

OPPOSITE PAGE: 'After the vicious Nazi attack on London last Wednesday (16th April 1941), all arguments against the evacuation of children have been settled in those areas badly blitzed, and nine times the usual number under the LCC evacuation scheme are now leaving London. An engine driver says "hello" to evacuees at a London station.'

OPPOSITE PAGE INSET: A group of London schoolgirls off to billets in Monmouth and Glamorgan. They were part of a contingent of 10,000 children evacuated on one single day from London and the Medway towns.

ABOVE TOP: Children at Waterloo Station to catch a train to the West Country are escorted by police.

ABOVE INSET: 'The British lion took a bow at the train window yesterday when this party of schoolgirls were being evacuated from the South-East coast to the west of England.'

RIGHT: This young boy is on his way to the West Country, one of many children who were originally evacuated to the countryside of south-east England but were relocated when the area became vulnerable to attack.

Settling in to new homes

Having never before experienced the quietness, the solitude or the animal life of the countryside, some children found their new surroundings disturbing. Conversely, others found a freedom and enjoyment they had not experienced in urban life roaming rural lanes and fields. Almost all, whatever their circumstances, grew to hold their host families in affection and many formed relationships which continued long after life returned to 'normal'. On both sides, there was a determination to 'make things work'; a way of contibuting to the war effort.

OPPOSITE PAGE TOP: 'Children making their way up a hillside agleam with flowers.' Taken in the first week of the evacuation, this picture intended to show the experience of life in the reception areas.

OPPOSITE PAGE INSET: Pictured in September 1942, before leaving for their new billets, the King family, Allen, Roy, Doris and Lydia, were chosen as 'model' evacuees to promote evacuation schemes.

OPPOSITE PAGE BELOW: Smiling children used to promote the benefits of evacuation. Taken after the first evacuees left their homes, it was intended to reassure the parents left behind and to encourage more people in safe areas to offer billets to evacuees.

RIGHT TOP: A notice broadcasting to parents the safe arrival of their children to an evacuation area.

RIGHT MIDDLE: Boys from Dulwich College sort out their luggage on arrival at their evacuation school in Tonbridge in Kent.

BELOW: 'A day with the evacuated children in the country. East End children and others enjoying the sunshine in Berkshire, reading letters from home.'

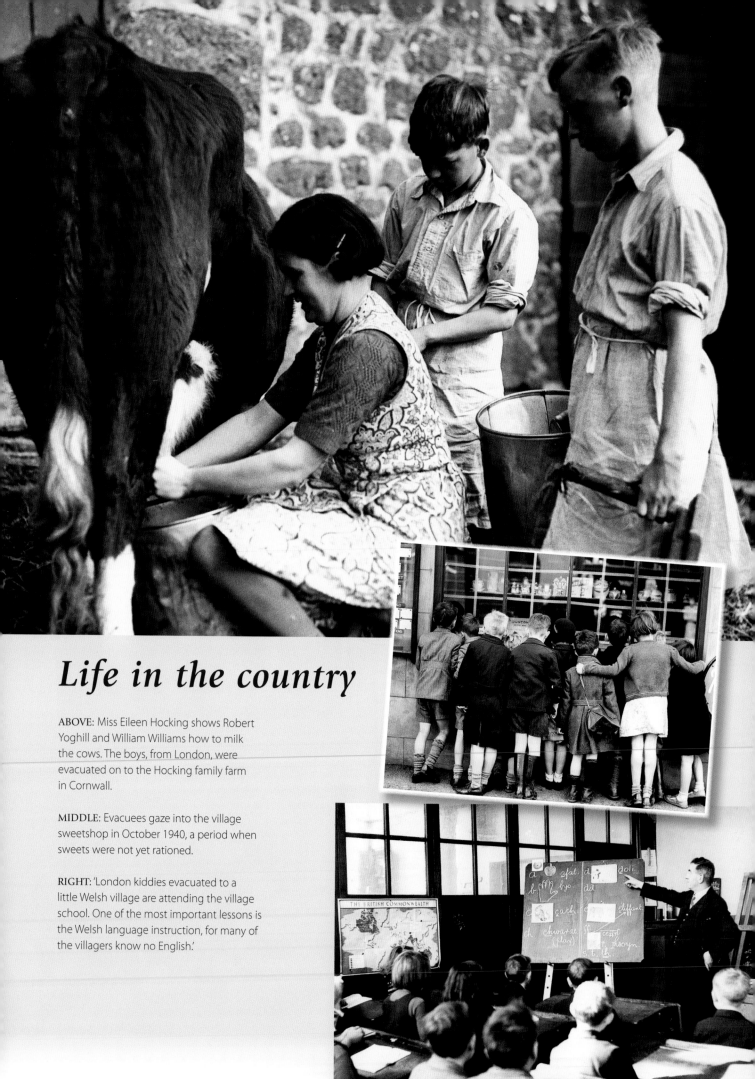

Life in the country

ABOVE: Miss Eileen Hocking shows Robert Yoghill and William Williams how to milk the cows. The boys, from London, were evacuated on to the Hocking family farm in Cornwall.

MIDDLE: Evacuees gaze into the village sweetshop in October 1940, a period when sweets were not yet rationed.

RIGHT: 'London kiddies evacuated to a little Welsh village are attending the village school. One of the most important lessons is the Welsh language instruction, for many of the villagers know no English.'

Working hard

Children contributed a great deal to the war effort. They helped their parents in the 'Dig for Victory' campaign by working in their gardens or allotments. They were also able to 'lend a hand on the land' by joining teams working on farms to boost food production.

Many of the 'drives' co-ordinated by the Womens Volunteer Service (WVS) relied on children's help with picking wild fruits and plants such as blackberries, crab apples, mushrooms and dandelion leaves. In something of a virtuous circle, children were also part of the teams collecting wild rosehips, which volunteers turned into rosehip syrup, a rich source of vitamin C, which was then given to children.

The WVS also ran 'salvage' drives, collecting door-to-door unused household items and waste. Children were also essential members of these drives, which provided some of the raw material for munitions.

TOP: Schoolboys from Eton on 'Long Leave' tending the allotments of members of the Eton Working Men's Allotment Society.

ABOVE: Children from London take part in a National Day of Prayer before setting off to the fields to help with hop picking.

LEFT: Schoolboys in Essex examine incendiary bombs which fell in their school grounds.

Reunited

OPPOSITE PAGE: Following weeks of separation since the children were evacuated to Saffron Walden from their home in Tottenham, the Elliott family were re-united in October 1939. Here, Mrs Elliott reserves a special hug for the youngest.

OPPOSITE PAGE INSET LEFT: Mrs Elliott runs to greet her six daughters.

OPPOSITE PAGE INSET RIGHT: The Elliott family are all together again.

RIGHT: A young girl searches her father's pockets for a treat in their first meeting for almost two months.

RIGHT INSET: In September 1944, these tired and weary travellers at Euston are part of the movement of returning evacuees. Unlike the coordinated and official process of evacuation, the return was much more low key. Families simply collected their evacuated children.

BELOW: The Good family returned to London after a five-year-long absence to find it much changed. Many families did not, or could not, return to their original homes but made a new life for themselves, often in areas to which they had been evacuated.

Running free

Many children were out of school for long periods and often they were unsupervised at home because Father was with the forces or working, and Mother was working as well. This led to a number of social problems. For example, there was an increase in vandalism and hooliganism. Public air-raid shelters were wrecked so many times by children that in the end they had to be kept locked, opened by the ARP warden when the alert sounded.

However, many children just enjoyed the freedom from continual adult scrutiny. They were free to play imaginary games and collect war 'souvenirs'. Bits of bombs and crashed planes were collected from bomb and crash sites and traded among children. This obviously unsafe activity was discouraged in varying degrees by adults.

OPPOSITE PAGE: Four boys take tea in the garden of their damaged home after a daylight raid in March 1943.

OPPOSITE PAGE INSET: Children from a London orphanage survey the wreckage of their home after it was hit during the Blitz.

RIGHT ABOVE: The child at play on the home-made cart calmly reads the danger notice.

RIGHT: After a particularly heavy raid on Coventry in April 1941, these schoolboys are given refreshments from a mobile canteen donated by the Americans.

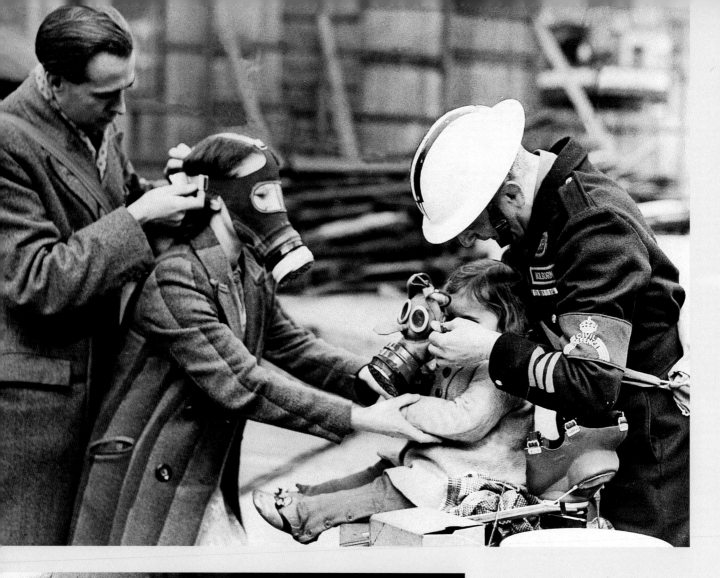

Protecting children

ABOVE: This little girl, Pat, was having her first gas mask fitted, comforted by her mother. Her red and blue mask had a 'nose' which made it look like the cartoon character Mickey Mouse.

LEFT: 'Wendy brings her gas mask to be repaired and points out the perished rubber and the small holes in the face piece.'

OPPOSITE PAGE TOP AND BELOW: In March 1941 there were concerns raised by the council in Dover suggesting an increase in the child population of the town. It is difficult to say whether this was a result of evacuee children in the area, or the fact that children had more free time and were less strictly supervised and so were more evident.

CHAPTER SEVEN

Business as usual

Although people on the home front lived
with the constant threat of invasion or aerial
attack and suffered the privations of rationing,
shortages and the blackout, there remained a
tremendous spirit in the British population. That
spirit manifested itself in a determination to
carry on as near as 'normal' a life as possible. Early
on in the war, the legend 'Business as Usual' was
seen chalked on many bombed-out shops; it
became a slogan for everyone.

Keeping up morale

The government capitalised on the positive public mood and boosted morale by promoted the idea of working together to defeat the enemy. Most propaganda campaigns emphasised social responsibility – 'Careless talk costs lives', 'Dig for victory', 'Women, join the factories', 'Do not waste food' – a far cry from the campaigns of the Great War which presented the Germans, or 'the Hun', as evil. Even simple things like donating pots, pans and garden railings to salvage drives encouraged the feeling of being able to contribute directly to the war effort.

More subtly, the presentation of attractive, glamorous young men and women working together in factories, army camps, airbases or on ships implied a British way of life under threat from Hitler and well worth protecting.

ABOVE: Capturing the humour of ordinary people, the notice painted on the side of this shelter suggests, perhaps ironically, that a night sheltering in an air raid is as entertaining as an evening in the music hall.

LEFT: The proprietor of this boot repair shop in Battersea was called up in the first week of the war and leaves a note for his customers on his plans for reopening.

OPPOSITE PAGE: This street fruit seller boasts that his oranges have come through Musso's (Mussolini's) 'Lake' – a nickname for the Mediterranean. He also has bananas for sale – a rarity during the war, especially by the time of the Blitz when this picture was taken.

'Keep smiling through'

Public morale was closely monitored. Without public support the prosecution of a war by a demoractic nation is difficult to sustain. Thus, there was government resistance when people first started sheltering in the Underground. Initially anxious to avoid a 'deep shelter mentality' in which fearful citizens spent all their time underground, the government eventually conceded when it was clear that this was not the case. Other government strategies, such as keeping in place production of items such as cosmetics and chocolate and sanctioning extra rations at special times like Christmas, kept morale high; in the words of Vera Lynn's song, the majority of the population did 'keep smiling through', often with comic good humour.

OPPOSITE PAGE TOP LEFT: 'An amusing offer seen in London after a bomb had demolished a dwelling house.'

OPPOSITE PAGE TOP RIGHT: Although a somewhat gruesome sight, this picture, taken in London towards the end of the Blitz, is a vivid demonstration of the of the fact that the severe bombing campaign had not brought about public pressure for the government to sue for peace with Germany.

OPPOSITE PAGE BELOW: 'British humour prevails through weeks of air raids: a comic police notice. Many street notices in London testify to the fact that in spite of the air raids British people are smiling through with characteristic humour. Here is a policeman's effort in the London area, warning passers-by to pass by quickly in a danger zone.'

RIGHT TOP: The signs on this ARP shelter offer a humourously defiant challenge.

RIGHT BELOW: An ironic message for the milkman from the residents of this Hackney street: 'Don't leave any milk'.

Entertainment

Entertainment was an important area for keeping up morale. When war was declared venues for public entertainment, such as cinemas, theatres, concert halls and football grounds, were closed down to avoid the possibility of many people being killed in a direct hit on a crowded area. When no bombing came many reopened with air-raid precautions in place.

Cinema was one of the most popular forms of public entertainment, with huge audiences for Hollywood movies such as *Gone With the Wind*. Despite the war, the British film industry also carried on, producing work ranging from Laurence Olivier's *Henry V* to news and public information films and documentaries like Roy Boulting's *Desert Victory*, shot during the battle for El Alamein.

RIGHT: With the majority of young men in the forces, the young women at this open-air dance at Brockwell Park, London, partner each other.

BELOW: Shoppers and stallholders in Lambeth Walk carry on with 'business as usual' after a raid in the early days of the Blitz.

The BBC

It was as source of immense pride for the BBC that it never failed to transmit its programming throughout the war. As the only broadcaster at the time, the BBC carried the burden of providing both a reliable news service and morale-boosting entertainment. At the outbreak of war the company axed its embryonic television channel and all radio stations except for one. This single station was essential for morale during the war. Not only did the public feel they were getting a fair news picture, the BBC also broadcast programmes that became national institutions. Popular programmes, drawing millions of listeners, included *The Brains Trust*, *Woman's Hour*, *Children's Hour*, *Forces' Favourites*, and *Music While You Work*. However, the most popular programme was *ITMA* (*It's That Man Again*), starring Tommy Handley. *ITMA* was a comedy sketch programme which made fun of everyone involved in the war, from Hitler to the Home Guard.

RIGHT TOP: Members of the Home Guard are rewarded with a concert, sponsored by the *Daily Mail*, at the Royal Albert Hall.

RIGHT MIDDLE: A close-up of the crowd at the Home Guard concert. While BBC Radio broadcast music on programmes such as *Forces' Favourites* and *Music While You Work*, live entertainment like this concert was rarer and much appreciated.

RIGHT BELOW: A Home Guard unit leaves a London cinema after a group outing.

Keeping the nation fed

Another strategy the government employed to promote the idea of a community spirit was the rationing system, which provided fair shares for all. It did not matter how rich you were, everyone got the same official ration. Additionally, prices of rationed and unrationed goods were strictly controlled to avoid profiteering. Apart from the capacity for the rich to buy more expensive, specially tailored clothing, it was generally not possible to buy something no one else could afford, unless it was purchased on the 'black market'. Even the Royal Family rationed themselves and stuck to the recommended five-inch-deep bath once a week to save fuel.

OPPOSITE PAGE TOP: This picture of a London street market during the first weeks of the war was published to promote the idea that there was no shortage of food and to try to prevent shortages occuring as a result of panic buying.

OPPOSITE PAGE BELOW LEFT: Queuing for a 'British Restaurant', a system of restaurants, each serving up to 500 meals a day, where for 1s 2d (6p) it was possible to buy a good-quality three-course meal. These meals were 'off the ration' and provided a valuable addition to the standard allocation, as well as saving customers valuable time, and fuel, by cooking their main meal of the day.

OPPOSITE PAGE BELOW RIGHT: The menu at a British Restaurant. This particular London restaurant extended its opening hours to serve hot meals to those, like firewatchers and ARP wardens, on duty at night.

BELOW INSET: Mrs Ramsey, a 72-year-old London resident, receives her 3501st cup of tea in Holborn tube station, where she frequently sheltered from air raids. In some of the larger shelters canteens serving hot meals were set up.

BELOW: A factory canteen. As the war progressed facilities for workers improved to include, in the larger factories, canteens serving hot food over and above the ration.

Fire of London

LEFT TOP AND MIDDLE: Workers walk to work past the fire tenders and burnt-out buildings on Monday, 30th December 1940, the morning after the raid that caused the second Fire of London.

BELOW: 'Outside their fire-wrecked office the staff of a City firm queue up to draw their weekly pay. A small table was the cashier's "office". On the ground lay a blackened typewriter – yesterday's glimpse of the "carry-on" City.'

OPPOSITE PAGE TOP: Following the fire Blitz on Sunday, 29th December 1940, soldiers help City clerks salvage books and files. The attack would create hours of painstaking work for the clerks as business records were checked and reconstituted.

OPPOSITE PAGE BELOW RIGHT: The Lord Mayor of London inspects books salvaged from the damaged Guildhall Library.

OPPOSITE PAGE BELOW LEFT: Workmen labour to provide a temporary roof to the Guildhall. Although the ancient walls remained relatively intact, the medieval building lost its roof in the fire.

Getting to work

ABOVE: On foot, by car or by bicycle, workers in a northern suburb of London head for their places of employment on Sunday, 26th May 1940, as they answer a call for a 'seven-day -a-week output effort'.

MIDDLE: Signs in Lambeth Walk point to the fact that this bomb-damaged thoroughfare is closed to traffic but shops are open for business.

LEFT: As petrol rationing bites, City office workers hitch a lift with the few motorists who do have petrol for their cars.

OPPOSITE PAGE TOP: The Ministry of Transport instituted a new river boat service between Westminster and Woolwich. Petrol rationing meant the more public transport could be used the greater the saving and the more smoothly the capital would run.

OPPOSITE PAGE BELOW: Travellers could buy tickets on board the river boat service but people with 'tickets for the relative land journeys may use them'. The river boat service helped remove road congestion caused by Blitz debris and eased the strain on the bomb-damaged bus stock.

CHAPTER EIGHT

Road to victory

The war is referred to as a 'world war' but for the first two years the conflict was largely confined to Europe, although Britain's position as a colonial power meant troops from the vast reaches of the British Empire served in her armies. When Italy declared war on Britain on 10th June 1940, the war spread to North Africa. As part of the Axis Powers, Italy was intent on occupying land in North Africa as part of a plan to contol the Mediterranean; It already dominated the northern shore. The Eighth Army, the 'Desert Rats', led the attempt to keep the countries of North Africa free from Axis occupation. Britain and its allies had much to lose if Germany and Italy succeeded in commanding the southern shore of the Mediterranean; British-controlled areas such as Malta and Gibraltar would almost certainly fall into Axis hands.

By June the following year another fighting front had

opened as Hitler, desperate for more resources, launched 'Operation Barbarossa', an attack on the USSR. In August 1939 Stalin had a non-aggression pact with Germany; many cite this as a principle reason why Germany felt secure enough to launch its invasion of Poland, the act that precipitated the war. Britain and Russia became allies, Churchill pledging British support to the Russian attempt to repel invading German forces. However, German blitzkrieg tactics proved useless in the USSR; the German Army found progress slow and battles in the harsh Russian winter conditions gruelling. Millions died in sieges of major Russian towns like Stalingrad (now Volgograd) and Leningrad (now St Petersburg).

In the early years, while Britain had stood largely alone, the USA had provided moral and practical support in the form of food and weapons. The Lend-Lease Agreement allowed Britain to obtain weapons and equipment

without having to pay immediately – items were lent for the duration of the war, to be paid for after the war was won. Although President Roosevelt was sympathetic, there was no real appetite for America to commit troops to the fighting.

That stance changed when the Japanese attacked the US naval base at Pearl Harbor, Hawaii, on 7th December 1941; another theatre of war opened, this time in the Pacific.

Thus, as 1942 commenced the conflict had engulfed much of the world. There was conflict in the Pacific, Russia and North Africa, as well as Europe where it had all started. The two sides were clearly drawn – the Allies: Britain, its colonies and those remnants of European countries that had managed to escape occupied Europe, the USSR and the USA; against them the Axis Powers: Germany, Italy and Japan. The road to victory was to be a slow and staged journey.

German surrender

From France in the west, from Russia in the east and from Italy and Greece in the south, German troops were pushed back into home territory throughout 1944 and into 1945. German towns and cities suffered some of the most devastating air raids of the war; thousands were killed, but the destruction of weapons production and infrastructure enabled the Allies to secure the upper hand. Last-ditch efforts in the Battle of the Bulge and attempts to attack Britain with the new pilotless bombs, the V1s and V2s, were not enough for Germany to wrest the initiative. In the face of defeat and as the Red Army took control in the ruined streets of Berlin, Hitler committed suicide on 30th April 1945. Field Marshal Keitel signed Germany's unconditional surrender on 8th May and the victory and peace in Europe was secure.

ABOVE: Crowds meet in Piccadilly Circus to hear the news of the final surrender of Nazi Germany.

RIGHT: On 8th May 1945, crowds wait patiently in Whitehall for the official announcement that 'This is VE Day'.

OPPOSITE PAGE TOP: 7th May 1945 and people gather outside Downing Street, spilling into Whitehall as they wait for news of Germany's final surrender. Although German troops had surrendered following Hitler's suicide on 30th April, the final signature on a declaration of unconditional surrender was not yet forthcoming.

OPPOSITE PAGE MIDDLE: 8th May and crowds line Parliament Street waiting for Winston Churchill's announcement from the balcony of the Ministry of Health and the commencement of VE Day celebrations.

OPPOSITE PAGE BELOW: As the celebrations gather momentum the Australian flag is carried. Although fighting continued in the Pacific, VE Day was a time of joy for all the Allied nations.

Peace in Europe

Although the peace began officially at one minute past midnight on 9th May 1945, the celebrations started on Tuesday, 8th May and went on throughout the night. The entire country celebrated in the streets, but London was the focus of the biggest festivities. Crowds had gathered in Whitehall, waiting for an official announcement of peace in Europe. The announcement was expected at 9.00 a.m. on the 8th May but it was not until 3.00 p.m. that Prime Minister Winston Churchill broadcast to the nation, the news relayed through loudspeakers in the centre of London. He said that the war in Europe would end at midnight, and praised the British people and their allies, but he also reminded them that Japan was not yet defeated.

OPPOSITE: Silence in Trafalgar Square as the crowds listen to the relay of Prime Minister Winston Churchill's broadcast announcing the official end to war with Germany and a public holiday – VE Day.

OPPOSITE PAGE TOP: Westminster is thronged with people, just some of of the 50,000 who celebrated in London on VE Day.

OPPOSITE PAGE BOTTOM: Crowds bring traffic to a standstill in Piccadilly Circus.

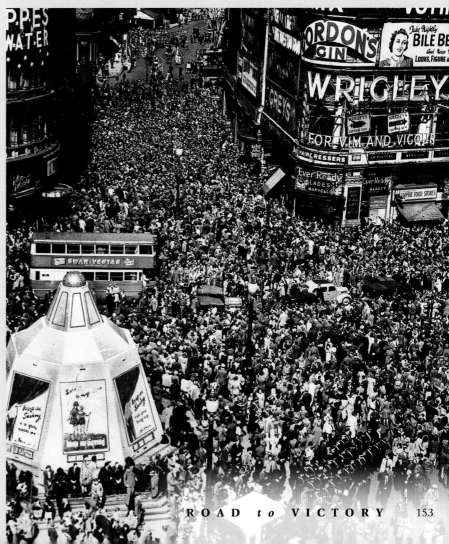

Celebrations

Churchill's broadcast was the signal for the party to begin throughout Britain. In central London around 50,000 revellers thronged the streets, many making their way to Buckingham Palace, calling for the King and Queen who, with their daughters, Princesses Elizabeth and Margaret, and Winston Churchill, appeared eight times on the royal balcony to acknowledge the crowd's joy. Celebrations continued as darkness fell and licensing laws were suspended for the night. Although everyone knew that the war was not over and the war in the Pacific continued, there was unrestrained joy after more than five and a half years of danger, deprivation and loss. The following Sunday, attendance at prayers of thanksgiving throughout Britain was so great that in many churches the services had to be relayed by loudspeaker to those outside.

ABOVE: ATS and American soldiers cheer from one of the plinths in Trafalgar Square.

BELOW: 8th May 1945 was a warm sunny day, reflecting the mood of the nation, and this group was one of many to paddle in the Trafalgar Square fountains.

OPPOSITE PAGE: In Piccadilly Circus, adventurous revellers climb the protective shell around the statue of Eros.

Street party!

MAIN PICTURE: At this street party in Hunslet, Leeds, national flags provide the bunting and a victory sign is chalked on the cobbles as the residents gather to celebrate.

OPPOSITE PAGE INSET: The residents of Kentwell Close in Brockley, south London, organised this children's party on VE Day.

BELOW: 'Street tea parties celebrate "V" Whitsun. Not everybody went from London to the seaside and other places this Whitsun (21st May 1945). Some preferred to stay at home like these residents of Tilloch Street, Islington, who organised tea parties in the street for the children, complete with paper hats and decorations.'

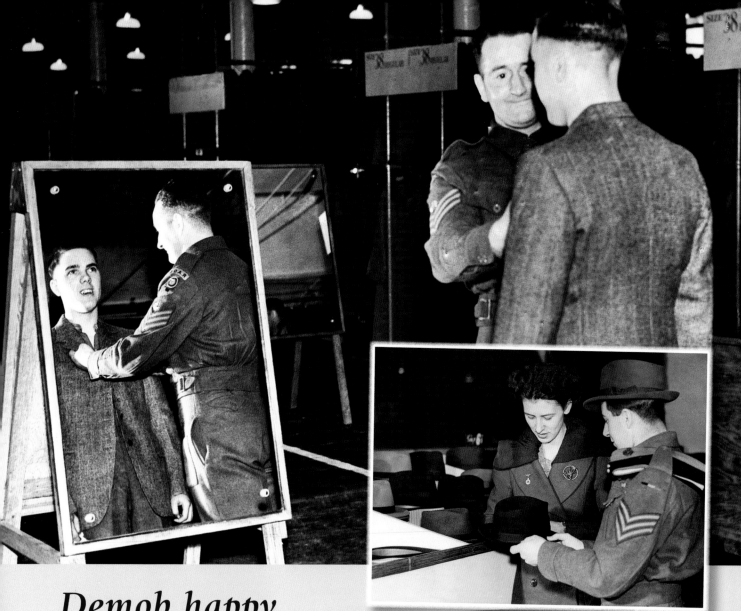

Demob happy

ABOVE: After the war ended millions of men had to be demobilised and the British military aimed to complete the paperwork for each man in 10 minutes; it was essential to avoid a backlog in order to make the return to 'Civvy Street' as smooth as possible. Here an ex-soldier tries on one of the millions of off-the-peg suits produced for demobbed men to prepare them for their peacetime roles.

ABOVE INSET: Here help is offered on that most important fashion accessory of the period – a hat.

RIGHT: A soldier is issued with pay, ration books, identity cards and health card, all part of the paperwork that was needed for life outside the military.

OPPOSITE PAGE ABOVE RIGHT: Being measured for a demob suit. Many men had been in service for the duration and had not had new civilian clothing for years. Their clothing entitlement is outlined on the sign.

OPPOSITE PAGE BELOW RIGHT: Private H. Salter, being measured here, is the first man to claim a 'non-austerity discharge suit'. Austerity Regulations had come into effect in March 1942. Clothing styles which used valuable materials merely for show were not permitted; so double-breasted jackets, turn-ups on trousers and decorative buttons were banned.

By the time Private Salter was ready for discharge in October 1944, the war was going well enough for the regulations to be relaxed.

OPPOSITE PAGE BELOW LEFT: Here is a happy Private Salter with his complete demob outfit.

Peacetime

Fifty-five million of the world's citizens had lost their lives in the conflict and throughout Europe the long process of reconstruction began. Britain faced years of austerity as it worked to pay the financial costs of the war. The nation had to turn its economy and industry from a single-minded focus on the war effort to more diverse peacetime production. However, it took time; rationing continued for a further nine years, indeed in some instances became more severe – bread was rationed even though it never had been during wartime.

As millions of men and women were demobilised from the armed forces and evacuees returned home, families and communities had to learn to live together in peacetime social structures that were, in many ways, very different to those in existence before 3rd September 1939.

AND AWAIT TO BE MEASURED

YOU ARE ENTITLED TO

1 SUIT.   1 TIE.
1 RAINCOAT. 1 HAT.
1 SHIRT.   1 Pʳ SHOE
2 COLLARS. 2 Pʳˢ SOCK

YOU WILL SERVE YOURSELF.

CIVILIAN EXPERTS AR
RE TO ASSIST YO

First published by Atlantic Publishing in 2011
Reprinted 2014

Atlantic World
38 Copthorne Road
Croxley Green
Hertfordshire, WD3 4AQ

Paperback ISBN 978-0-9558298-8-8
Hardback ISBN   978-1-909242-50-0

Printed and bound in China

BIBLIOGRAPHY

The People's War by Angus Calder, pub: Panther

How We Lived Then by Norman Longmate, pub: Hutchinson

Living Through the Blitz by Tom Harrisson, pub: Penguin

Children of the Blitz by Robert Westall, pub: Macmillan

The Blitz Then and Now (2 Volumes) ed. Winston Ramsay,
pub: After the Battle Publications

Blitz on Britain 1939–1945 by Alfred Price, pub: Sutton
Publications

Bombers and Mash by Raynes Minn, pub: Virago

War Papers introduced by Ludovic Kennedy, pub: Collins

Life on the Home Front by Tim Healey, pub: Readers Digest

Chronicle of the Twentieth Century edited by Derrick Mercer
pub: Longman

ACKNOWLEDGEMENTS

The photographs in this book are from the archives of
the *Daily Mail*.
That this book can be published is a tribute to the
dedication of the staff, past and present, in the Picture
Library at Associated Newspapers. Particular thanks to
Steve Torrington, Alan Pinnock and Dave Sheppard